Holiday

JAZZ CHANTS®

CAROLYN GRAHAM

OXFORD

UNIVERSITY PRESS

Oxford University Press

198 Madison Avenue
New York, NY 10016 USA

Great Clarendon Street
Oxford OX2 6DP England

Oxford   New York

*Athens Auckland Bangkok Bogota Buenos Aires Calcutta Cape Town
Chennai Dar es Salaam Delhi Florence Hong Kong Istanbul Karachi
Kuala Lumpur Madrid Melbourne Mexico City Mumbai Nairobi Paris
São Paulo Singapore Taipei Tokyo Toronto Warsaw*

and associated companies in
Berlin   Ibadan

OXFORD is a trademark of Oxford University Press.

ISBN 0-19-434927-6

Copyright © 1999 Oxford University Press

Editorial Manager: Shelagh Speers
Senior Editor: Sherri Arbogast
Developmental Editor: Marilyn Rosenthal
Production Editor: Joseph McGasko
Elementary Design Manager: Doris Chen Pinzon
Designer: David Hildebrand
Senior Art Buyer: Alex Rockafellar
Art Buyer: Tracy Hammond
Production Coordinator: Shanta Persaud
Production Manager: Abram Hall

Illustrations by Carolyn Croll, Catherine Rose Crowther, Liisa Chauncy Guida,
Anne Kennedy, Susan Miller, Kathleen Rogers, Doug Roy/Square Moon,
and Ted Williams

Cover Design by Doris Chen Pinzon
Cover Calligraphy by Don Grimes
Cover Illustrations by Ted Williams

Printing (last digit): 10 9 8 7 6 5 4 3 2 1

Printed in Hong Kong.

 Dedicated with love to Burçu Bulak and Pepsi

Table of Contents

Unit 1: January - New Year's Day

Holiday Chant 10

New Year's Dream ♪ 12

New Year's Resolutions 14

Unit 2: February - Valentine's Day

You're My Valentine ♪ 16

Funny Valentines 17

One, Two, I Like You ♪ 18

I Sent a Valentine to Sue 19

Unit 3: March - St. Patrick's Day

Green Jeans ♪ 21

I Saw a Leprechaun 22

The Irish Are Coming ♪ 23

Things That Are Green 24

Unit 4: April - Easter

Easter Colors 26

Here Comes the Easter Bunny ♪ 27

How Many Eggs in the Easter Basket? ♪ 28

Easter Eggs, Pink and Blue 30

Unit 5: May - Mother's Day

Good Morning, Mama ♪ 32

Mother, Mommy, Mama, Mom ♪ 33

Mama Bird Takes Care of Her Babies ♪ 34

Mother's Day Plans 35

Today Is Mother's Day 36

Unit 6: June - Father's Day

Good Morning, Papa ♪ 38

Father, Daddy, Papa, Dad ♪ 39

Father's Day Party ♪ 40

Today's the Day ♪ 42

The Third Sunday in June 43

Unit 7: July - The Fourth of July

Red, White, and Blue 45
All Dressed Up 46
Marching, Marching, Here They Come! 47
I Love the Fourth of July ♪ 48

Unit 8: August - Summer Fun

Skateboard, Water Skis, Surfboard, Wow! 51
Beach Ball Boogie ♪ 52
Hop in the Car ♪ 54

Unit 9: September - Back to School

The First Day of School ♪ 57
Good-bye, Summer. Hello, Fall. ♪ 58
Fall Colors 59
Everybody's Back in School ♪ 60

Unit 10: October - Halloween

Halloween Colors 63
Halloween Parade 64
Trick or Treat 65
Witches, Witches ♪ 66

Unit 11: November - Thanksgiving

What Did the Chicken Say on Thanksgiving Day? ♪ 69
Baby Turkey Chant 70
Native American Chant 71
Wishbone Chant 72
Today's Thanksgiving Day! 73

Unit 12: December - Christmas

Christmas Colors, Christmas Sounds 75
What Do You Want for Christmas? 76
Christmas Candy. Yum, Yum, Yum! 77
Santa Claus Is on His Way ♪ 78
Christmas Cards ♪ 80

Teacher's Notes

What is *Holiday Jazz Chants*?

Holiday Jazz Chants by Carolyn Graham is a collection of 50 songs and chants about the major holidays celebrated in the United States. The songs and chants presented in this book focus on vocabulary, expressions, and language functions used in connection with each holiday. Colorful illustrations reinforce the meaning of the targeted language by depicting the situations and cultural icons most often associated with each holiday.

The holidays in this book are grouped according to the calendar months, with one holiday featured in each "unit." For example, the songs and chants for the January unit are about New Year's Day, and the songs and chants in the February unit are about Valentine's Day. In August and September, however, seasonal themes are featured instead of specific holidays. August is presented as the "summer fun" unit, since summer and summer vacations best characterize this month in the minds of most Americans, and "school" is the theme for September, since the new school year begins in September in most American schools.

Each holiday's songs and chants can be used during the entire month of the holiday. You can use them as preview, review, or simply as a way of conveying the spirit of each holiday to your students.

Songs are indicated in the Table of Contents by a musical note next to the title, and musical notation is provided for each song.

The *Holiday Jazz Chants* Cassette/Compact Disc

All of the songs and chants are recorded and are available on cassette or compact disc (CD). The recording, which uses children's voices, is useful for providing the underlying rhythm of the songs and chants and for providing a model for students to follow.

Suggestions for Presenting the Songs and Chants

Step 1
Preview the name of the holiday and any of the vocabulary in the song or chant that is associated with that holiday, using illustrations to support your instruction whenever possible.

Step 2
Play the recording once or twice to allow students to become familiar with the words and rhythm of the chant or the melody of the song. Some of the song melodies are traditional ones that students may be familiar with. Encourage students to tap out the rhythm as they listen to the song or chant.

Step 3
Teach the song or chant line by line. With their books still closed, students should repeat each line after you. You can use the recording to model each line if you prefer. Some teachers teach the song as a chant first, and then present it with its melody. **Note:** The symbols (✷) that appear in some of the chant lines represent claps.

Step 4
Have students open their books. Play the recording again. Have students read along with the text silently at first so that they can begin associating the rhythm and intonation of the song or chant with the words printed on the page. Play the recording again. This time, have students chant or sing along with the recording (as a whole class).

Step 5
Once students are comfortable with the song or chant, create various performance arrangements for them. For example, if a chant is interactive (that is, has questions and answers, like a dialogue), divide the class into two groups and have each group take the role of a speaker. Here is an example using the chant *What Do You Want for Christmas?*:

Group 1: What do you want for Christmas?
Group 2: (clap) I want a football.

For songs or chants that are divided into two or more verses, you can assign a verse to each group, and have them stand when it is their turn to perform. There are many possibilities; allow your students to help you create interesting arrangements for the songs and chants, including combinations of solos, pairs, and small groups.

Some songs and chants lend themselves well to gestures or mime. Lead your students with gestures whenever possible, as it will make the experience more natural and fun, especially for younger or more shy students. Also, encourage students to bring in percussion instruments (especially ones from their own cultures) such as tambourines, maracas, or bells.

Extending and Reinforcing the Language in the Songs and Chants

There are many activities you can do to extend and reinforce the language presented in the songs and chants. A few examples follow.

"Personalize" the Songs and Chants

Students enjoy songs and chants even more when they have created them themselves. Whenever possible, substitute students' real information in the song or chant. For example, in the chant *New Year's Resolutions*, there are lines such as "I promise (clap, clap) to make my bed each day; I promise (clap, clap) to put my things away." Elicit similar sentences from the students about promises they will make for their New Year's resolutions, and arrange these sentences into a chant:

Student 1: I promise (clap, clap) to help my little sister.
Student 2: I promise (clap, clap) to feed the cat each morning.

When students create their own songs and chants, don't insist that all the lines rhyme. Rhymes do make the song or chant easier to memorize, but they can sometimes be more difficult to create.

"Cloze" the Songs and Chants

A "cloze" activity is one in which students have to fill in blanks or come up with a missing word or phrase. This activity can be done orally or in writing. One way to do it is to sing or chant part of a line, stop, and have students sing or chant the remainder of the phrase. Here is an example using the song *Good Morning, Mama:*

Teacher: Good morning, Mama. I want to say…
Students: Happy Mother's Day!

Another way to do it is to replace a word in the middle of a sentence or phrase with a clap, and then elicit the word from the students after you've completed the sentence or phrase.

Teacher: Good morning, Mama. I (clap) to say…
Students: Want.

"Chunk" the Language of the Songs and Chants

A language "chunk" is a word or phrase that is isolated from a larger segment. Select certain vocabulary, idioms, or phrases from the body of the song or chant and create new arrangements with the language. Here is an example using selected language chunks from the song *Father, Daddy, Papa, Dad*:

Group 1: Father, Father, Father, Father. He's my Father. (clap, clap, clap)
Group 2: Daddy, Daddy, Daddy, Daddy. He's my Daddy. (clap, clap, clap)

Groups 3 and 4 do the same thing respectively with the words "Papa" and "Dad." Have the four groups take turns chanting their parts. If desired, have each group chant their lines louder and louder each time. As a variation, have two groups alternate their lines:

Group A: Father
Group B: Daddy
Group A: Father
Group B: Daddy
Groups A and B: He's my father. (clap, clap, clap) *or* He's my daddy. (clap, clap, clap)

Role Play and Movement with the Songs and Chants

Many learners can retain new language better when they associate movement with it. Certain songs and chants will lend themselves well to activities involving movement. The class can do the movements together, or you can assign roles to particular students, who will then dramatize these roles while the rest of the class is chanting or singing. Using the chant *Marching, Marching, Here They Come!* as an example, have the entire class march as if they are members of a marching band. Select certain students to act out particular roles: band leader, baton twirler, trumpet player, tuba player, etc. Another idea is to divide the class into five groups and assign each group an instrument from the chant. As their assigned instruments are mentioned, the members of the group stand and "play" them (i.e., try to imitate the sounds).

Have Students Share Their Own Cultures

Encourage students to share holiday celebrations from their own cultures. Try to create songs and chants that are built around these holidays. Base the new songs and chants on the models provided in this book, on your own ideas, or on student-generated ideas. If the students can bring in music or musical instruments that are associated with their holidays, incorporate these elements as much as possible.

Structure Key

Structure	Chant or Song	Page
Articles: **Definite/Indefinite**	New Year's Dream	12
	Green Jeans	21
	I Saw a Leprechaun	22
	Father's Day Party	40
	I Love the Fourth of July	48
	The First Day of School	57
	What Did the Chicken Say on Thanksgiving Day?	69
	What Do You Want for Christmas?	76
Conditional Clauses	New Year's Dream	12
	Funny Valentines	17
	Christmas Cards	80
Future	Funny Valentines	17
	I Saw a Leprechaun	22
	Mother's Day Plans	35
	Today Is Mother's Day	36
	I Love the Fourth of July	48
	Trick or Treat	65
	Christmas Cards	80
Imperative Statements	Marching, Marching, Here They Come!	47
	Skateboard, Water Skis, Surfboard, Wow!	51
	Beach Ball Boogie	52
	Hop in the Car	54
	Trick or Treat	65
Infinitives	New Year's Resolutions	14
	Mother's Day Plans	35
	Father's Day Party	40
	Trick or Treat	65
Past Tense	I Sent a Valentine to Sue	19
	I Saw a Leprechaun	22
	What Did the Chicken Say on Thanksgiving Day?	69
	Wishbone Chant	72
	What Do You Want for Christmas?	76

Structure	Chant or Song	Page
Plurals	You're My Valentine	16
	Green Jeans	21
	The Irish Are Coming	23
	Mama Bird Takes Care of Her Babies	34
	All Dressed Up	46
	Marching, Marching, Here They Come!	47
	Fall Colors	59
	Halloween Colors	63
	Halloween Parade	64
	Christmas Colors, Christmas Sounds	75
Possessives	Father's Day Party	40
	Halloween Colors	63
Possessive Adjectives	New Year's Resolutions	14
	You're My Valentine	16
	Green Jeans	21
	Mother, Mommy, Mama, Mom	33
	Mama Bird Takes Care of Her Babies	34
	Mother's Day Plans	35
	Father, Daddy, Papa, Dad	39
	Today's the Day	42
	All Dressed Up	46
	Skateboard, Water Skis, Surfboard, Wow!	51
	Witches, Witches	66
Present Tense: Third Person	Funny Valentines	17
	Things That Are Green	24
	The Third Sunday in June	43
	All Dressed Up	46
	Everybody's Back in School	60
	Today's Thanksgiving Day!	73
Present Continuous Tense	The Irish Are Coming	23
	Red, White, and Blue	45
	Hop in the Car	54
	Everybody's Back in School	60
	Halloween Parade	64
	Santa Claus Is on His Way	78
Present Perfect Tense	New Year's Dream	12
	I Saw a Leprechaun	22

JANUARY

SUN.	MON.	TUES.	WED.	THURS.	FRI.	SAT.
					1	2
3	4	5	6	7	8	9
10	11	12	13	14	15	16
17	18	19	20	21	22	23
24	25	26	27	28	29	30
31						

Holiday Chant

January's here!
* Hooray!
Happy, Happy New Year's Day.

February's here!
* Hooray!
Happy, Happy Valentine's Day.

March is here!
* Hooray!
* Have a nice St. Patrick's Day.

April's here!
* Hooray!
The Easter Bunny's coming!
Have a wonderful day.

May is here!
* Hooray!
Happy, Happy Mother's Day.

* = clap

June is here!
* Hooray!
Happy, Happy Father's Day.

July is here!
* Hooray!
The Fourth of July!
Have a wonderful day.

August is here!
* Hooray!
* Have a wonderful holiday.

September's here!
* Hooray!
Back to school!
Have a wonderful day.

October's here!
* Hooray!
Halloween's coming!
Have a wonderful day.

November's here!
* Hooray!
* Have a nice Thanksgiving Day.

December's here!
* Hooray!
Santa Claus is coming!
Have a wonderful day.

New Year's Dream

Melody: Auld Lang Syne

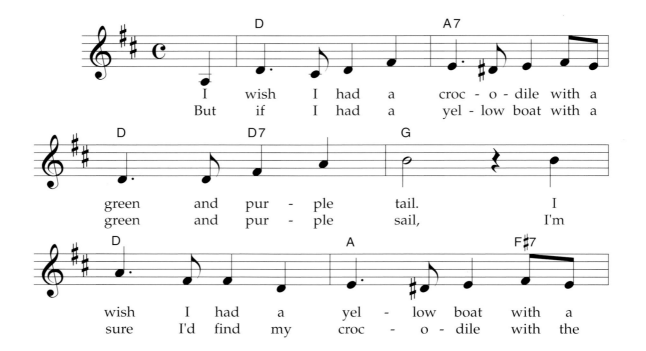

I wish I had a croc - o - dile with a
But if I had a yel - low boat with a

green and pur - ple tail. I
green and pur - ple sail, I'm

wish I had a yel - low boat with a
sure I'd find my croc - o - dile with the

green   and   pur - ple   sail.   I've   nev - er   seen   an
green   and   pur - ple   tail.   We'd   sail   a - round   the

oct - o - pus.   I've   nev - er   seen   a   whale.   I've
o - cean   blue.   We'd   sail   a - round   the   sea.   We'd

nev - er   seen   a   croc - o - dile   with   a
sail   and   sail   a - round   the   world,   my

green   and   pur - ple   tail.
croc - o - dile   and   me.

New Year's Resolutions

I promise * * to be very, very good.
I promise * * to do the things I should.
I promise * * to make my bed each day.
I promise * * to put my things away.
I promise not to throw my socks on the floor.
I promise * * to put my socks in the drawer.
I promise * * to do my homework right.
I promise not to stay up late at night.
I promise to listen to my mom and dad.
I promise not to do anything bad.

FEBRUARY

SUN.	MON.	TUES.	WED.	THURS.	FRI.	SAT.
	1	2	3	4	5	6
7	8	9	10	11	12	13
14	15	16	17	18	19	20
21	22	23	24	25	26	27
28						

TO MY VALENTINE

You're My Valentine

I like ti-gers, I like cats, but you're my val-en-tine.

I like ze-bras, I like bats, but you're my val-en-tine.

I like croc-o-diles, I like frogs, I like din-o-saurs, I like dogs.

I like but-ter-flies, I like bees, but you're my val-en-tine. (yeah, yeah, yeah)

I like but-ter-flies, I like bees, but you're my val-en-tine.

Funny Valentines

Boys are silly.
Girls are smart.
I love you
with all my heart.

Boys are noisy.
Girls are, too.
You like me,
and I like you.

Mama loves coffee.
Papa loves tea.
I love my teacher,
and my teacher loves me!

The birds won't sing,
the stars won't shine,
if you won't be
my valentine.

One, Two, I Like You

One, two, I like you. One, two,
I like you. One, two, three, you like me and
I like you. One, two, I like you.
One, two, I like you. One, two, three,
you like me and I like you. (I do!)

I Sent a Valentine to Sue

I sent a valentine to Sue.
She sent a valentine to you.
You sent a valentine to Lee,
but you didn't send one to me!

I bought a valentine for Bill.
He bought a valentine for Jill.
She bought a valentine for Sue,
but she didn't buy one for you!

I made a valentine for Kim.
She made a valentine for Lee.
He made a valentine for you,
but he didn't make one for me!

MARCH

SUN.	MON.	TUES.	WED.	THURS.	FRI.	SAT.
	1	2	3	4	5	6
7	8	9	10	11	12	13
14	15	16	17	18	19	20
21	22	23	24	25	26	27
28	29	30	31			

Green Jeans

He's wear-ing green jeans —— and a

bright green shirt. She's wear-ing a long green sweat-er and a

short green skirt. He's got an ap-ple for the teach-er in a

lit-tle green box. He's wear-ing big green sneak-ers with his

big green socks. She's wear-ing lit-tle green gloves and a

big green hat. She's got a kel-ly green rib-bon on her

kel-ly green cat. They're eat-ing green pop-corn.

Hoo-ray! —— To-day's St. Pat-rick's Day! ——

I Saw a Leprechaun

I saw a leprechaun hiding in a tree.
I saw a leprechaun and he saw me.
I said, "I've never seen a leprechaun before!"
He said, "You probably won't see one anymore."

I saw a leprechaun hiding in a tree.
I saw a leprechaun and he saw me.
I saw a leprechaun peeking in my door.
He said, "I've never seen a boy before!"

The Irish Are Coming

Melody: The Irish Washerwoman

Oh, the I-rish are com-ing, the I-rish are sing-ing. The
Oh, the I-rish are com-ing, the I-rish are sing-ing. Their

I-rish are laugh-ing, their church bells are ring-ing. The
drum-mers are drum-ming, their church bells are ring-ing. Their

I-rish are com-ing, they're all wear-ing green. The
child-ren are danc-ing, they're all wear-ing green. The

I-rish are march-ing on March sev-en-teen!
I-rish are march-ing on March sev-en-teen!

Things That Are Green

The trees are green.
The grass is green.
My clothes are green.
My nose is green.

Your chair is green.
Your hair is green.
Everything's green
on March seventeen!

His hat is green.
Her cat is green.
His plants are green.
Her pants are green.

Our house is green.
Their mouse is green.
Everything's green
on March seventeen!

APRIL

SUN.	MON.	TUES.	WED.	THURS.	FRI.	SAT.
				1	2	3
4	5	6	7	8	9	10
11	12	13	14	15	16	17
18	19	20	21	22	23	24
25	26	27	28	29	30	

Easter Colors

Pink and white, pale yellow,
Pale green, deep purple.
Pink and white, green and yellow.
These are the colors of Easter.

Pink and white Easter bunny.
Green and yellow Easter basket.
Deep purple, shiny ribbon.
These are the colors of Easter.

Pink and white Easter bunny.
Green and yellow Easter basket.
Pink and purple Easter eggs.
These are the colors of Easter.

Here Comes the Easter Bunny

How Many Eggs in the Easter Basket?

col - or are the eggs in the East - er bas - ket? Look in the East - er bas - ket! One is pink, one is pur - ple. One is green, one is yel - low. One is pink and green and pur - ple. Eggs in the East - er bas - ket!

Easter Eggs, Pink and Blue

Easter eggs, pink and blue.
One for me, one for you.

Easter eggs, one, two, three.
One for you, two for me!

Easter eggs, pink and blue.
One for me, two for you.
Easter eggs, one, two, three.
Two for you and one for me!

One for you, one for me.
One for the teacher.
One, two, three!

I ♥ my mommy

MAY

SUN.	MON.	TUES.	WED.	THURS.	FRI.	SAT.
						1
2	3	4	5	6	7	8
9	10	11	12	13	14	15
16	17	18	19	20	21	22
23	24	25	26	27	28	29
30	31					

Good Morning, Mama

Mother, Mommy, Mama, Mom

Moth - er, Mom - my, Ma - ma, Mom.
Moth - er, Mom - my, Ma - ma, Mom.

Moth - er, Mom - my, Ma - ma, Mom. She's my moth - er.
Moth - er, Mom - my, Ma - ma, Mom. She's my moth - er.

She's my mom - my. She's my ma - ma.
She's my mom - my. She's my ma - ma.

1.
She's my mom.

2.
She's my mom.

Mama Bird Takes Care of Her Babies

Ma - ma bird_____ takes
Ma - ma cat_____ takes
Ma - ma dog_____ takes

care of her ba - bies._____ Ma - ma bird_____ takes
care of her kit - tens._____ Ma - ma cat_____ takes
care of her pup - pies._____ Ma - ma dog_____ takes

care of her ba - bies._____ Ma - ma bird_____ takes
care of her kit - tens._____ Ma - ma cat_____ takes
care of her pup - pies._____ Ma - ma dog_____ takes

care of her ba - bies,_____ and my ma - ma takes
care of her kit - tens,_____ and my ma - ma takes
care of her pup - pies,_____ and my ma - ma takes

care of me. Oh,
care of me. Oh,
care of me.

Mother's Day Plans

What are you going to give your mother?
What are you going to buy for your mom?
Where are you going to go?
What are you going to say?
What are you going to do on Mother's Day?

Papa's going to give her flowers.
My brother's going to give her a pet.
What are you going to do?
I don't know.
I haven't decided yet.

Today Is Mother's Day

Today is Mother's Day.
Let's help Mama.
I'll make breakfast.
You make lunch.
I'll do the dishes.
You do the shopping.
Let's help Mama.
It's Mother's Day.

Today is Mother's Day.
Let's help Mama.
I'll sweep the bedrooms.
You make the beds.
I'll clean the kitchen.
You do the laundry.
Let's help Mama.
It's Mother's Day.

JUNE

SUN.	MON.	TUES.	WED.	THURS.	FRI.	SAT.
		1	2	3	4	5
6	7	8	9	10	11	12
13	14	15	16	17	18	19
20	21	22	23	24	25	26
27	28	29	30			

To Dad

Good Morning, Papa

Father, Daddy, Papa, Dad

Fath - er,	Dad - dy,	Pa - pa,	Dad.		
Fath - er,	Dad - dy,	Pa - pa,	Dad.		

Fath - er, Dad - dy, Pa - pa, Dad. He's my fath - er.
Fath - er, Dad - dy, Pa - pa, Dad. He's my fath - er.

He's my dad - dy. He's my pa - pa.
He's my dad - dy. He's my pa - pa.

1.
He's my dad.

2.
He's my dad.

Father's Day Party

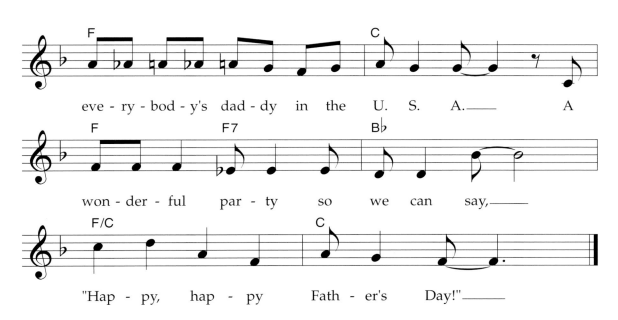

eve - ry - bod - y's dad - dy in the U. S. A.——— A

won - der - ful par - ty so we can say,———

"Hap - py, hap - py Fath - er's Day!"———

41

Today's the Day

The Third Sunday in June

When is Father's Day?
    * I know.
    It's the third Sunday in June.
    It's not the second Sunday in August,
    it's the third Sunday in June.
    It's not the first Sunday in April,
    it's the third Sunday in June.
    It's not the fourth Sunday in July.
    Oh, no!
    It's the third Sunday in June.

Is it the first Sunday in June?
    No!
Is it the second Sunday in June?
    No!
Is it the third Sunday in June?
    Yes! It's the third Sunday in June!

Red, White, and Blue

Fourth of July.
Red, white, and blue.
Hamburgers, hot dogs, chicken, too.
Fourth of July.
Red, white, and blue.
Everybody's coming to the barbecue!

Listen to the firecrackers!
Look at the sky!
My little dog hates the Fourth of July.
Fourth of July.
Red, white, and blue.
Everybody's coming to the barbecue!

All Dressed Up

His sweater is red.
His socks are blue.
His shirt is white.
His pants are, too.
His hat is covered with stars.
Oh, my!
He's all dressed up
for the Fourth of July!

Her dress is red.
Her socks are, too.
Her dog is wearing
red, white, and blue.
Her jacket is covered with stars.
Oh, my!
She's all dressed up
for the Fourth of July!

Marching, Marching, Here They Come!

Marching, marching, here they come!
Here comes the marching band.
Left, right, left, right.
Here comes the marching band.
Listen to the trombones. Here they come!
Here comes the marching band.
Listen to the trumpets. Here they come!
Here comes the marching band.

Trombones, trumpets, clarinets!
Here comes the marching band.
Listen to the tubas! Listen to the drums!
Here comes the marching band.
Left, right, left, right.
There goes the marching band.
Left, right, left, right.
There goes the marching band. Wow!

I Love the Fourth of July

Melody: Stars and Stripes Forever

I love the Fourth of Ju - ly with the
I love the Fourth of Ju - ly. Da, da,

flags and the bands and the mu - sic.
da, da, da, da, da, da, da, da.

I love to look at the sky on the fourth day of Ju -
I love to look at the sky. Ba, ba, ba, ba, ba, ba,

ly. (two, three, four) Here on the Fourth of Ju - ly you and
ba. (two, three, four) Here on the Fourth of Ju - ly you and

I will be march - ing to the mu - sic.
I will be march - ing to the mu - sic.

I love the Fourth of Ju - ly. I love the
I love the Fourth of Ju - ly. I love the

flags, I love the bands, I love the mu - sic.
flags, I love the bands, I love the mu - sic.

AUGUST

SUN.	MON.	TUES.	WED.	THURS.	FRI.	SAT.
1	2	3	4	5	6	7
8	9	10	11	12	13	14
15	16	17	18	19	20	21
22	23	24	25	26	27	28
29	30	31				

Skateboard, Water Skis, Surfboard, Wow!

Skateboard, water skis, surfboard, wow!
Hop on your skateboard, let's go now.
Skateboard, water skis, surfboard, wow!
Put on your water skis, let's go now.

Skateboard, water skis, surfboard, wow!
Hop on your surfboard, let's go now.
Skateboard, water skis, surfboard, wow!
Let's go, let's go, let's go now!

Hop on your skateboard, stay on the sidewalk.
Hop on your surfboard, catch the wave.
Hop on your skateboard, put on your water skis.
Hop on your surfboard, catch the wave!

Skateboard, water skis, surfboard, wow!
Let's go, let's go, let's go now!

Beach Ball Boogie

Beach ball boo-gie.   Throw it,   catch it.

Beach ball boo-gie.   Throw it,   catch it.   Beach ball boo-gie.

Throw it a-round.——   Please don't drop that beach ball!——

Base-ball boo-gie.   Throw it,   catch it.   Base-ball boo-gie.

Throw it,   catch it.   Hit it hard,—— and

run, run, run.   Please don't drop that base-ball!——

Bas-ket-ball boo-gie. Throw it,   catch it.   Bas-ket-ball boo-gie.

Throw it,   catch it.   Grab it,   drib-ble it, and

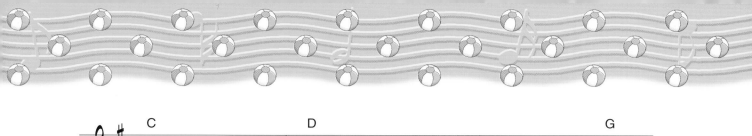

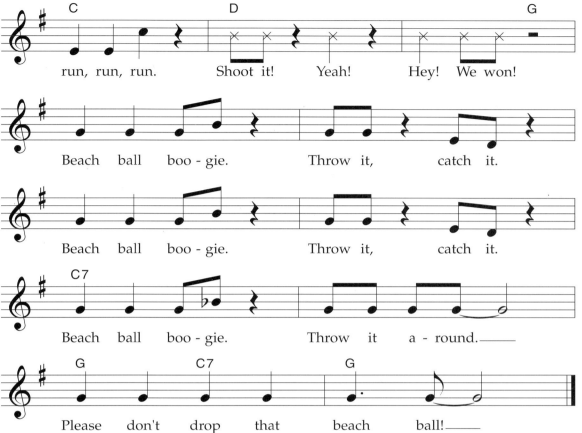

run, run, run. Shoot it! Yeah! Hey! We won!

Beach ball boo - gie. Throw it, catch it.

Beach ball boo - gie. Throw it, catch it.

Beach ball boo - gie. Throw it a - round.

Please don't drop that beach ball!

Hop in the Car

No, not yet.   Are we   there   yet,   Dad - dy?

No, not yet.   Are we   there   yet,   Dad - dy?

No, not yet,   but we're   al - most   there. Hoo - ray!

SEPTEMBER

SUN.	MON.	TUES.	WED.	THURS.	FRI.	SAT.
			1	2	3	4
5	6	7	8	9	10	11
12	13	14	15	16	17	18
19	20	21	22	23	24	25
26	27	28	29	30		

The First Day of School

Oh, it's the first hour___ of the first lesson___ of the first day of school.

Oh, it's the first ho - ur of the first lesson___ of the first day of school.

Oh, it's the first min - ute of the first ho - ur of the first day of school.

Oh, it's the first sec - ond of the first min - ute of the first day of school. Hoo - ray!

Good-bye, Summer. Hello, Fall.

Good-bye, summer. Hel-lo, fall.——

Good-bye, base-ball. Hel-lo, home-work. So long, sum-mer, sit-

ting in the sun. Hav-ing fun,—— do-ing noth-ing.

Good-bye, sum-mer, learn - ing how to skate. So long, sum-mer,

sleep-ing late. No more sum-mer,—— that's all!——

Good - bye, sum - mer. Hel - lo, fall!——

Fall Colors

Fall colors.
Look at the trees.
Red and gold
autumn leaves.

Leaves falling, falling down,
autumn leaves, all around.
Leaves falling, falling down.
Red and gold on the ground.
Autumn leaves, gold and brown.
Falling, falling, all around.

Green, red, gold, brown
autumn leaves, falling down.

Everybody's Back in School

Eve - ry - bod - y's back in school to - day.____ Eve -

ry - bod - y's back in school.____ The

prin - ci - pal's back.____ The teach - ers are back.____ Eve -

ry - bod-y's back in school.____ The jan - i - tor's back,____

sweep - ing the halls.____ The bus driv - er's back on the bus.__

Eve - ry - bod - y's back in school to - day.____ Eve -

ry - bod-y's wait - ing for us.____ Eve - ry - bod - y's back in

school to - day.____ The gym teach - er's back in the gym.__

The mu-sic teach-er's back in school to-day.— Eve-

ry-bod-y's wait-ing for him.— Eve-ry-bod-y's back in

school to-day.— The swim-ming teach-er's back in the pool.—

— Eve-ry-bod-y's back from their sum-mer va-ca-tion.—

Eve-ry-bod-y's back in school.—

OCTOBER

SUN.	MON.	TUES.	WED.	THURS.	FRI.	SAT.
					1	2
3	4	5	6	7	8	9
10	11	12	13	14	15	16
17	18	19	20	21	22	23
24	25	26	27	28	29	30
31						

Halloween Colors

Black cat.
Orange pumpkin.
White ghost.
Green-eyed monster.
Black, orange, white, green.
These are the colors of Halloween!

Black cats.
Witches' hats.
Jack-o'-lanterns.
Jack-o'-lanterns.
Black, orange, white, green.
These are the colors of Halloween!

Halloween Parade

Black cats, here they come!
Black cats, one by one.
Leaping, howling, having fun.
Black cats, here they come!

Skeletons dancing, here they come!
Skeletons dancing, one by one.
Shaking, rattling, having fun.
Skeletons dancing, here they come!

Witches flying, here they come!
Witches flying, one by one.
Witches on broomsticks, having fun.
Witches flying, here they come!

Spiders crawling, here they come!
Spiders crawling, one by one.
Creeping, crawling, having fun.
Spiders crawling, here they come!

Trick or Treat

Trick or treat.
Trick or treat.
I want something good to eat.
Trick or treat.
Trick or treat.
Give me something nice and sweet.
Give me candy and an apple, too.
And I won't play a trick on you!

Witches, Witches

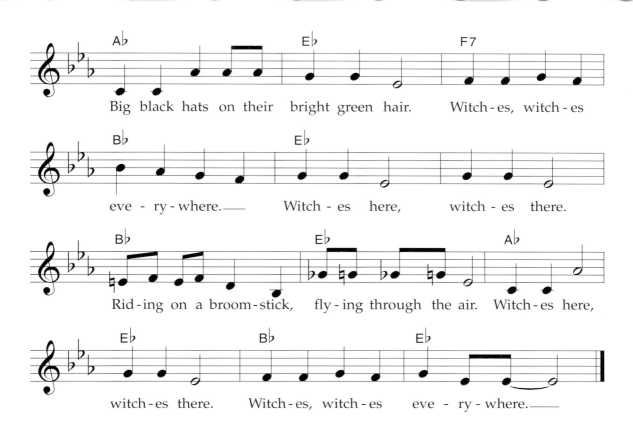

Big black hats on their bright green hair. Witch-es, witch-es

eve-ry-where.—— Witch-es here, witch-es there.

Rid-ing on a broom-stick, fly-ing through the air. Witch-es here,

witch-es there. Witch-es, witch-es eve-ry-where.——

NOVEMBER

SUN.	MON.	TUES.	WED.	THURS.	FRI.	SAT.
	1	2	3	4	5	6
7	8	9	10	11	12	13
14	15	16	17	18	19	20
21	22	23	24	25	26	27
28	29	30				

What Did the Chicken Say on Thanksgiving Day?

What did the chick-en say on
What did the rab-bit say on
What did the tur-key say on

Thanks-giv-ing Day?_____ What did the chick-en say on
Thanks-giv-ing Day?_____ What did the rab-bit say on
Thanks-giv-ing Day?_____ What did the tur-key say on

Thanks-giv-ing Day?_____ The chick-en said, "Hey,_____ I'm
Thanks-giv-ing Day?_____ The rab-bit said, "Hey,_____ I'm
Thanks-giv-ing Day?_____ The tur-key said, "Hey!_____ It's

glad I'm not a tur-key._____ I'm glad I'm not a tur-key_____ on
glad I'm not a tur-key._____ I'm glad I'm not a tur-key_____ on
tough to be a tur-key._____ It's tough to be a tur-key_____ on

Thanks - giv - ing Day."_____
Thanks - giv - ing Day."_____
Thanks - giv - ing Day!"_____

Baby Turkey Chant

Fiddle-faddle.
Diddle-daddle.
Mama Turkey.
Gobble-gobble.

Fiddle-faddle.
Diddle-daddle.
Baby Turkey.
Beep! Beep! Beep!

Fiddle-faddle.
Diddle-daddle.
Papa Turkey.
Gobble-gobble.

Fiddle-faddle.
Diddle-daddle.
Baby Turkey.
Beep! Beep! Beep!

Native American Chant

Mohawk, Navajo, Cherokee, Sioux.
  Mohawk, Navajo, Cherokee, Sioux.

Mohawk, Navajo, Cherokee, Sioux.
  Mohawk, Navajo, Cherokee, Sioux.

Kickapoo, Mohawk,
  Kickapoo, Mohawk.
Kickapoo, Mohawk,
  Kickapoo, Mohawk.

Mohawk, Navajo, Cherokee, Sioux.
  Mohawk, Navajo, Cherokee, Sioux.

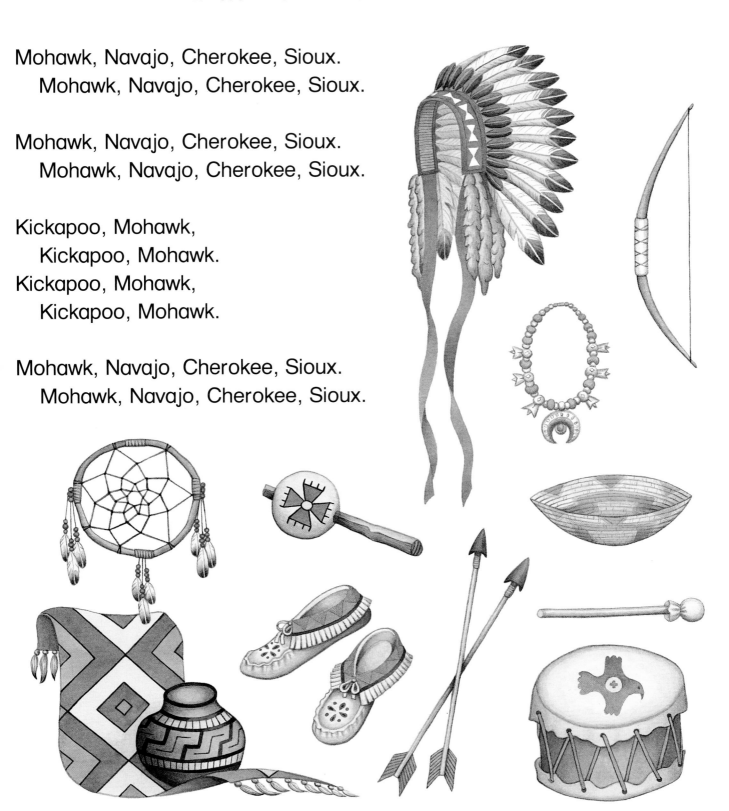

71

Wishbone Chant

Wishbone, wishbone.
Who got the wishbone?
Wishbone, wishbone.
Who got the wishbone?
   I got the wishbone!
Good for you!
I hope you get your wish.
   I do, too.

Wishbone, wishbone.
Who got the wishbone?
Wishbone, wishbone.
Who got the wishbone?
   I got the wishbone.
Good for you!
I hope you get your wish.
   I do, too!

Today's Thanksgiving Day!

Today's Thanksgiving Day!
Today's Thanksgiving Day!
The turkey's in the oven.
The table's set.
Today's Thanksgiving Day!

The peas and carrots are ready.
The cranberry sauce is here.
The pumpkin pies look wonderful!
Today's Thanksgiving Day!

   Is the turkey ready?
No, not yet.
   Is the turkey ready?
No, not yet.

The turkey's ready.
Here it comes!
Today's Thanksgiving Day! Hooray!

DECEMBER

SUN.	MON.	TUES.	WED.	THURS.	FRI.	SAT.
			1	2	3	4
5	6	7	8	9	10	11
12	13	14	15	16	17	18
19	20	21	22	23	24	25
26	27	28	29	30	31	

74

Christmas Colors, Christmas Sounds

Bright red, dark green.
These are the colors of Christmas.
Red stockings, green trees.
These are the colors of Christmas.

Gold ribbon, silver bells,
colored lights on the Christmas tree.
Silver, gold, red, and green.
These are the colors of Christmas.

Bells ringing, children singing.
These are the sounds of Christmas.
Children playing, Santa laughing.
These are the sounds of Christmas.

Bells ringing, children singing.
Santa laughing, children playing.
Ringing, singing, laughing, playing.
These are the sounds of Christmas.

What Do You Want for Christmas?

What do you want for Christmas?
   * I want a football.
What do you want for Christmas?
   * I want a baseball.
What do you want for Christmas?
   * I want a basketball.
What do you want for Christmas?
   I want a pair of skis.

Football, baseball, basketball, skis.
Football, baseball, basketball, skis.

What did you get for Christmas?
   * I got a beach ball.
What did you get for Christmas?
   * I got a bowling ball.
What did you get for Christmas?
   * I got some golf balls.
What did you get for Christmas?
   I got a pair of skis.

Christmas Candy. Yum, Yum, Yum!

Christmas candy.
  Yum, yum, yum!
Christmas cookies.
  Yum, yum, yum!
Christmas fruitcake.
  Yum, yum, yum!
Mistletoe, mistletoe!
  Kiss, kiss, kiss!
Christmas morning.
  Lots of toys.
Christmas stockings
  for girls and boys.
Christmas carols.
  Tra, la, la!
Mistletoe, mistletoe!
  Kiss, kiss, kiss!

Santa Claus Is on His Way

San - ta Claus is on his way.——— He's com - ing.———

San - ta Claus is on his way.——— He's com - ing———

here to - day——— on his sleigh.——— Jin - gle bells are ring - ing. San -

ta Claus is sing - ing.——— San - ta Claus is on his way.———

He's com-ing. San-ta's com-ing here to-day.

Eve-ry-bod-y knows it's

Christ-mas 'cause San-ta Claus is on his way

to-day. San-ta Claus is on his way!

Christmas Cards

Melody: Jingle Bells

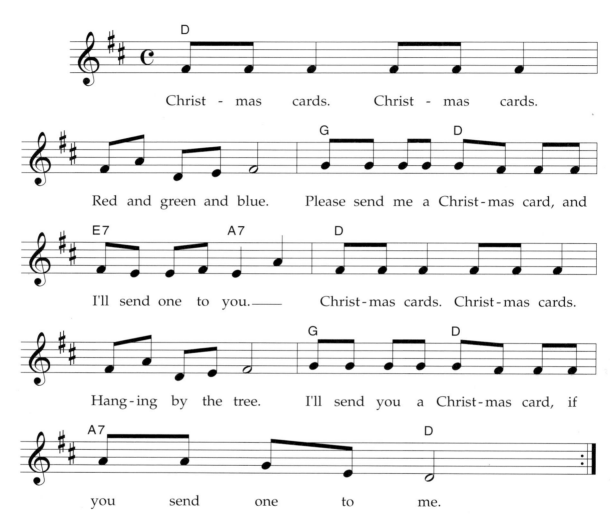

Christ - mas   cards.   Christ - mas   cards.

Red and green and blue.   Please send me a Christ-mas card, and

I'll send one to you.——   Christ-mas cards. Christ-mas cards.

Hang-ing by the tree.   I'll send you a Christ-mas card, if

you   send   one   to   me.

80